A MOTHER'S HEART

Mulenga Chanda

Grosvenor House
Publishing Limited

This book is published by
Grosvenor House Publishing Ltd
Link House
140 The Broadway, Tolworth, Surrey, KT6 7HT.
www.grosvenorhousepublishing.co.uk

A CIP record for this book
is available from the British Library

ISBN 978-1-78623-496-4

DEDICATION

I would like to dedicate this book to someone special; my biological mother, for being a great example of what it takes to hold on to God.

FOREWORD

Meeting hundreds of children who have no one to call mum is nothing less than a travesty! I am a mother to hundreds of orphans and abandoned children at our King's Children's home in Kenya as well as being the biological mother to a little red-head seven year old boy called Josiah!

Sometimes when we don't have biological children we can be fooled into thinking we aren't mothers, but the reality is, every one of us have people looking up to us. People are looking to you, longing that you would take them under your wing, selflessly pouring your time and love into them. You are called to have relationships that help to nurture and nourish those around us. The maternal instinct is one which God invested into the lives of women. We are gentle natured but incredibly fierce protectors. We are compassionate and wise when correcting and guiding and our influence can never be underestimated.

As mothers, whether biological or spiritual, we have to first acknowledge the heart of God over our lives and then from this truth we are able to love more completely. Some days we might be tired and our tolerance and grace levels can feel somewhat diminished. Through this book, Mulenga, beautifully redirects us back to the source: God! He is our comfort, our joy, our wisdom, our strength and the foundation of all love. Only in true dependency on God can we truly flourish in this critically important role and become the "Mother" He has called us to be.

Becky Murray
Author of "Mother Bumala"
One By One

CONTENTS

I was on my way to an appointment and, whilst on the train, God dropped the idea of this book into my spirit. It was such an audible thought that I commenced writing straight away. Whether you are a biological mum or a mother in the faith, this book will share principles that God has put in my heart to help strengthen and fulfil us on our journey. God's delight over mothers is immense. I hope that as we explore God's heart for women together in this book, you too will see why we are so treasured and identify the privileged position of a mother.

My heart is to inspire women everywhere with wisdom and insight into how you have been made.

CHAPTER 1

THE VALUE OF A MOTHER

The family unit has existed from the beginning of time. The Trinity is a beautiful example of how the family flourishes when all members play their part. The Father, Son and Holy Spirit dwell in perfect harmony because they each know who they are and what their purpose is – love. 'God Himself is love' *(1 John 4:8)*. 'God chose to make us in His image and likeness' *(Genesis 1:27)*, therefore we are made in love. You may not have realised this before, but your primary purpose on earth is to be loved and to give love. God shows us our identity and purpose by creating us in love.

The way that a family loves each other, then, is of utmost significance to God, and He leads us by His example which we will explore in this book.

Similarly, our parents are one of the biggest examples of love for us. They raise us right from the moment we are born through to adulthood, so a lot of us will have spent the majority of our time being influenced by them. Mothers in particular often have the predominant caregiving role generally speaking. You may not have known your biological mum or may have had a difficult relationship with her. I recognise that for any mother to be in a situation where they have forsaken or hurt their biological or spiritual children is a reflection of their own pain that may not have been dealt with or an inability to cope. If difficult feelings arise when reading this book, I encourage you to share them with a trusted friend, counsellor or God if you can. God uses the people around us to help us heal. He cares about the pain we experience and encourages us to process it: 'He will call on me, and I will answer him; I will be with him in trouble, I will deliver him and honour him' *(Psalm 91:15)*.

Oftentimes, a mother figure will be present in our lives in some form and will have helped shape us in different ways. This book is an exploration and celebration of the powerful, invaluable love that God designed every mother to behold.

We are all different in how we manage the various situations we find ourselves in. All of us can struggle and make mistakes, but our hope is in not giving up and trying over and over again with God's help. Such is the heart of a mother, never giving up but relentlessly believing that they will be able to make a difference if they keep going. Philippians 4:13 says: 'I can do all things through Christ who strengthens me'. The encouragement here to every mother is never to give up. And as the aim of relentless love stands for mothers, we too should never give up on our own mothers. Let's look at the bright side of the sacrifices they have made and continue to make and realise that a mother really is worth appreciating.

Mothers are often full of a spontaneous faith that they can still do something to make a difference, no matter how challenging the situation may be. I know that this confidence lies in the sovereignty of God according to Luke 3:5 *(King James Version)*: 'Every valley shall be filled, and every mountain and hill shall be brought low, and the crooked shall be made straight, and the rough ways shall be made smooth'. As mothers, we lay down our lives for our families in whatever capacity – we are worth our weight in gold.

As mothers, we often find ourselves in some of the most difficult and trying moments, yet we go out of our way to care, at the expense of our own needs a lot of times. I encourage each of us to think deeply about how much a mother loves and appreciate them. Mothers are known for putting their own interests aside to ensure someone else is cared for. Depending on the character, a mother may walk boldly defiant or with fear and fright but with one thing in common, the cry to make a difference. I call a mother's heart a heart of great tapestry that only the maker and the creator understands. A mother finds herself in that very unique position of being the person who can love, cry and forgive their child all in one breath and forget all the past pains and sorrows. A mother really is worth valuing because no amount of words will equate to the tremendous outpouring of love and affection towards their child, children, family, both immediate and extended.

A mother consistently cares in so many ways and that is why the word mother means the world to a lot of people. This goes for children in every category, not being essential how they find themselves in the arms of that mother. I believe children are to be embraced, whether young or old, biological or spiritual. Embracing gives children security and confidence, which encourages them to aspire to do more, thus making themselves more useful to the community and the world at large. When I look at and review the depth of a mother's love, I see no way of ending appreciating mothers. They are absolutely phenomenal individuals that I believe we can always seek to understand and be mindful of. This is why I am grateful for celebrations like Mother's Day. It creates and embeds a culture of everyone honouring their mothers, no matter what they may have gone through in their relationship. Even where there may be some who might still want to ignore the day, it will be brought to their conscience that there is a need to value a mother or mother figure. The Bible says in the book of Ephesians that honouring mothers and fathers comes with a promise of things going well in your personal life, and long life to all who show honour to their mothers and fathers is promised: 'honour your father and mother' This is the first commandment with a promise: If you honour your father and mother, things will go well for you, and you will have a long life on the earth *(Ephesians 6:1–3)*.

The word 'honour' means to highly respect or regard. This is a very significant clue that God wants respect to be modelled throughout the household. He even says that: 'things will go well for you, and you will have a long life on the earth'. You may wonder why honour has such an impact on our wellbeing? Well, it's because honour promotes connection, and connection is vital to our quality of life because it builds self-worth. If you receive respect from someone over time, you are far more likely to have a strong connection with that person and greater self-esteem. Likewise, where we haven't had that experience we are far more likely to struggle. We are made for connection, both with God and with others. This is why it is so important for us to stay connected to God if we want to mother well. We need to keep receiving the love that the Father has for us to enable us to give it out in a healthy way. This is a journey. We all have made and will make mistakes along the way and that's ok. If we make honour and connection (with God and our families) our priority, we can experience the best relationships God intended for us.

Valuing ourselves

A Mother is an intricate individual who also needs a lot of care alongside those she is caring for. When a mother is cared for too, it enhances her ability to fulfil the many dreams and giftings God put inside of her. As women, we all have things that we struggle with, many of which can emanate from a lack of self-care, disconnection from God or unprocessed emotional pain. When we don't take care of ourselves we can get burnt out, resentful, short-tempered, irritable and our care for others can waver. God has created us to be powerful individuals, not powerless ones. Other people can contribute to our happiness, but fundamentally it is our own responsibility.

When our own sense of self-worth is being nurtured, we will naturally find it easier to take care of those around us. Not only is self-care essential to our own wellbeing, it is also a great example to model to our children and our communities.

What does self-care look like to you? What enables you to find rest, be uplifted or be fed?

Here are a few examples if you need them:

Carve out time in the day to do something you enjoy. Not something functional, something that nourishes you and your soul. A long soak in the bath perhaps, a shopping trip, a walk on your own, a creative activity or a beauty treatment. You may need to organise childcare if it helps you to get some time to yourself.

Journalling can be an integral part of self-care. It helps you to process your life situations, emotions and your walk with God. I believe it is important to journal regularly to really take care of yourself and function better. (If you would like to learn more about the benefits of journalling, I have written a book about it called *Capture the Moment*, Volume 1 why Journal & Capture The Moment, Volume II writing Journal which can be found on Amazon.com).

Sometimes self-care can involve making time to talk to trusted friends about what's going on in your life. As well as enjoying each other's company, it can be helpful to share emotional pain with a friend that you know well. 'The heartfelt counsel of a friend is as sweet as perfume and incense' *(Proverbs 27:9)*.

Make clear boundaries with your children about what you are and are not willing to do. Children will have more respect for their mothers when we are honest with them. Being honest and realistic about our capacity always helps to embed a great foundation of trust. It is important to recognise that the mother/child relationship is the development of such a vital relationship that becomes a model for all future relationships the child engages in. A mother's needs and feelings are just as important as a child's. Of coursemothers make many sacrifices, but ultimately, the relationship has to work for both the mother and the child in order for everyone to be their best self.

The Bible beautifully describes the heart of a mother in Proverbs 31:

10 She is worth far more than rubies.

11 Her husband has full confidence in her and lacks nothing of value.

12 She brings him good, not harm, all the days of her life.

13 She selects wool and flax and works with eager hands.

14 She is like the merchant ships, bringing her food from afar.

15 She gets up while it is still night; she provides food for her family and portions for her female servants.

16 She considers a field and buys it; out of her earnings she plants a vineyard.

17 She sets about her work vigorously; her arms are strong for her tasks.

18 She sees that her trading is profitable, and her lamp does not go out at night.'

My interpretation of this last verse is that no matter how tough it may be, the determined mother will rise to the challenge, waking up daily to fulfil the assignment of God over her life. A Mother's love is the fighting spirit that is driving a mother forward each time. Therefore, we need all the nourishment we can get; be it physical, spiritual or emotional.

'And let us not grow weary of doing good, for in due season we will reap, if we do not give up.' *(Galatians 6:9).*

Beloved, when you feel yourself become weary, take time to be restored.

CHAPTER 2

A MOTHER'S LOVE IS
BUILT ON GOD'S LOVE

'Faith, hope, and love abide, but the greatest of these is love'
(1 Corinthians 13:13).

It is clear that God created women with such giftings that we
need the strength and direction from God in our daily journeys.
As mothers, we need to pay particular attention to love: to dwell
in love, to move in love. God's love is the foundation on which
every mother's love was designed to be built. God has shown us
the essence of His love by an act of self-sacrifice – sending His one
and only son to the cross to pay the penalty for our sin. This
sacrificial act of love through the cross demonstrates that God
totally accepts us, because He was willing to enable us to be
forgiven for everything we have ever done. God not only accepts
and embraces us as we are, He also equips us by giving us the
Holy Spirit to dwell inside of us; enabling us to love just as
He loves. This love is unpacked in more detail in 1 Corinthians
13:4–8: 'Love is patient, love is kind. It does not envy, it does not
boast, it is not proud. It is not rude, it is not self-seeking, it is
not easily angered, it keeps no record of wrongs. Love does not
delight in evil but rejoices with the truth. It always protects,
always trusts, always hopes, always perseveres. Love never fails'

A mother finds herself in a position where she has the potential
to love unconditionally. All of us have hurts and genuine reasons
why we struggle to love at our fullest potential, yet at the same
time, the Holy Spirit can empower us through our pain and hurt
to love supernaturally. When we embrace the unceasing delight
and love of the Father for ourselves, we look less to those around
us to fulfil our needs and are able to love a lot more freely.
God does not expect perfection, but he rewards our sincere efforts
to love.

God our Father is in the business of restoration. We will always need His precious spirit to empower us whatever stage we are at, yet at the same time His longing is to restore and heal our wounds. God's heart is to bind up the broken-hearted, bring freedom to captives and release prisoners from darkness.

If you'd like to, you can take some time here to think about, pray through, write down any hurting parts of you that you would like God to heal...

Jesus further reminds us in the book of John: just as the father has loved me, so have I loved you *(John 15:9)*.

The flip side of this for me in relation to a mother's love is that just as God has loved us unconditionally, so mothers can be ready to love. It may seem hard, yet it is Jesus himself who gives us the assurance that we can do all things through Christ that strengthens us. Unconditionally meaning we don't love because we are expecting something in return, we give of love wholeheartedly and remain happy to be a blessing.

In essence, a mother needs to abide in the perfect love of the Father according to John 15:5 – 'I am the vine; you are the branches. Whoever abides in me and I in him, he it is that bears much fruit, for apart from me you can do nothing.

John 15:10 gives us a picture of what it looks like to abide in love: 'If you keep my commandments, you will abide in my love, just as I have kept my Father's commandments and abide in his love.'

To abide in Jesus means to keep his commandments and to keep his commandments means to love God with all our hearts and souls and minds and to love our neighbour as ourselves. Matthew 22:37–39:

'37And he said to him, "You shall love the Lord your God with all your heart and with all your soul and with all your mind".
38This is the great and first commandment.
39And a second is like it: "You shall love your neighbour as yourself".'

This leaves mothers with a mandate to stay in love, to Abide in God's love and therein operate from a place of love in how we respond to the different situations and circumstances that we countlessly find ourselves in. Our response should be tailored on God's love that is so intricately woven inside of us leaving us with an ability to make decisions based on God's love. What do I mean intricately woven? It's a love like no other that loves against all odds and a lot of times, leaves many wondering why and how?

When we operate from a foundation of love as mothers, we make right decisions leading to many untold great outcomes. When mothers make decisions from a position of love, all those looking up to them are influenced in a very positive way and the outcome has a great positive impact on society. Why do I say so? The honest truth is that the more people are loved genuinely, the more they are able to remain productive in their personal relationships thus having a positive ripple effect. It is quite clear that operating in love builds and strengthens relationships whatever the case may be.

When we operate according to the principles of God, we have a consequential feeling of satisfaction and fulfilment at making the right decision as instructed by God. There is no doubt that this leads to an inner peace and an unexplainable sense of joy and fulfilment following decisions made in love. There is no loss in remaining obedient to God by being a loving mother. Standing on God's word and responding in obedience to His word creates such wholesome attributes that are actually felt and admired from far. Operating and responding from a position of love helps mothers remain at peace with their loved ones. God gives mothers a perfect assurance He will be with them: 'Finally, brothers, rejoice. Aim for restoration, comfort one another, agree with one another, live in peace; and the God of love and peace will be with you' *(2 Corinthians 13:11)*.

A mother is needed to love and to guide in love thus bringing about restoration and comfort to many people around her.

When we look at the subject of love, there are many ways that we as mothers can sometimes feel like we can't give any more or do certain things, yet I am always reminded of the incomparable love of the father who gave everything that we might live in abundance. Beloved, there is always enough. We can always ask for more love and fresh filling. Love does not condemn *(John 3:16-17)*. In the same way, we as mothers are not to condemn our children or anyone in our care, but rather to hold them dear and to love them in spite of any challenges and by so doing, the love of God will be seen in us and through us as mothers. This verse also shows us that love has a very redeeming quality to it. Therefore, when we do mess up as mothers, our choices to love from there on in are so effective and have such redemptive power.

One way that we display our love for God is through our trust, prayer, and devotion to Him. The more we cultivate our relationship with God, the more we love Him and the easier it becomes to love our children and those looking up to us as their mother figure. We really abide through a genuine love for God, we pursue in love, we pray in love and we obey in love by total surrender to God. It is only when we have set this foundation of love in God that everything we give out flows through it and from it.

CHAPTER 3

A MOTHER COMFORTS

Mothers are often looked to as comforters. We have a natural, in-built ability to comfort, be it through physical touch, a listening ear or compassionate words, for example. For some this can feel more instinctive than others, but one thing is for sure, we can all feel like we reach our limit from time to time. We get tired, impatient, frustrated and just want to give up sometimes. But there is hope: God comforts us, so that we can keep comforting others. Isaiah 66:13 says: 'as one whom his mother comforts, so I will comfort you; you shall be comforted in Jerusalem'. God uses the example of how a mother comforts to show how He himself comforts us. Here is God helping us understand what His love looks like. He is a great comforter. He always knows just what we need.

If God, who is our comforter and the comforter can compare His comfort to that of a mother, it shows the level of trust that God has bestowed on us as mothers.

It is phenomenal that God would compare Himself to us. This comparison emphasises just what a relational God is. The Hebrew words of comfort used in this verse have the sense "to be sorry", "to help find release from pent-up sorrow and emotion" and to "give relief". The use of the word "comfort" in this verse is very insightful as it shows us that God empathises with whatever we're going through and wants to help us to process it. There is an increasing amount of evidence in psychological research which shows that in order to thrive in every area of our lives, we need to have our feelings heard, accepted and released in some way. In letting our feelings just "be", we are, in essence, communicating the message that "you are seen and accepted as you are", reaffirming our sense of worth and value. If we can do this for our loved ones, it will really emulate the unconditional love of the Father who accepted us all in our mess; sending Jesus to show us that.

Humans will show some big emotions. This can be really challenging for parents and can feel very overwhelming, but if we can remember the importance of empathy as the verse denotes, we can learn to work with people instead of against them. Emotional outbursts are the perfect opportunity to show that we are a safe place. Just as God is our refuge. It is then from that place of feeling heard and accepted that a child or adult can move forward in a healthy way.

I am reminded that a mother's comfort is truly so much like our Heavenly Father. God is always there to guide us and shepherd us through every situation we go through in life. The mother is often readily available to help, to build, to restore and obviously, in it all, be there to comfort a child at any point of their life. Mothers will often comfort, almost by default, as care or strengthening a loved one comes so naturally. In that assurance, the child keeps running back to the mother for this continuous guidance, care, support; being comforted through it all. There is an assured confidence that when a child goes to a mother figure in their life, they have hope. Look at how the psalmist describes this comfort:

Psalm 23:1–6
The Lord is my shepherd; I shall not want.
He makes me lie down in green pastures.
He leads me beside still waters.
He restores my soul.
He leads me in paths of righteousness for his name's sake.
Even though I walk through the valley of the shadow of death, I will fear no evil, for you are with me; your rod and your staff, they comfort me.
You prepare a table before me in the presence of my enemies; you anoint my head with oil; my cup overflows...

A Mother's comfort often brings with it a positive hope that the situation will turn around for the better. The psalm above describes some of the darkest moments a person can endure, yet through it all, God gives great assurance that His comfort will restore and protect us.

Many of us will know that generally life brings with it many, many challenges at every stage of growth and maturity. I know there are people who look at other families from the outside and think that life is all rosy for them. This is not the case. I have grown to understand that life throws all sorts of challenges to people. The most important thing to remember in the situations we face is to respond based on the comforting, counselling words we have received in God's promises.

Children of all ages, therefore, will have trials they are going through just by virtue of being here on earth. Yet we keep running to God for comfort and assurance that God will make a way; putting a smile back on our faces. Similarly, I believe as a mother, we have a responsibility to ensure that we remain peace carriers as best as we can; comforting and bringing hope to the "children" around us who have such a need for a support and guidance.

I understand that at times, children behave in a way we do not expect them to behave. We as God's children, sometimes do not behave in the way God would like us to behave – but one thing I know is that God never gives up on us. In the same way, we should never give up on anyone despite their issues, despite how hard their turn around may look, but rather, just as God has comforted us, that we ourselves will be able to comfort the other person.

2 Corinthians 1:3–4: 'Blessed be the God and Father of our Lord Jesus Christ, the Father of mercies and God of all comfort, who comforts us in all our affliction, so that we may be able to comfort those who are in any affliction, with the comfort with which we ourselves are comforted by God.'

Sometimes the experiences people may be facing can look impossible to resolve, but I would like to encourage you to never write anyone off because of what they are going through. It is in these moments when we need to position ourselves to give the best comfort we can because we know that God will bring the turn around. The psalmist says in Proverbs 21:31: 'The horse is made ready for the day of battle, but victory rests with the Lord'.

It is our duty, through God's strength, to bring hope to people by comforting them. There are many ways that we can comfort and a powerful way is to give our children examples of how God has been faithful in comforting us. It doesn't matter how hard the situation may be, a soft, wise answer will always bring a smile to someone's face; offering peace and security. You may never know the impact that you can have on someone's life. It could just be that one word of comfort that brings healing and fulfilment to a son or daughter's heart. Where there is comfort, there lies an assurance for the person in need that there is hope for them. This can make individuals feel secure enough to be vulnerable and keep seeking support. An avenue for comfort is then created bringing restoration and hope from God. The psalmist says in Psalm 23:4: 'Even though I walk through the valley of the shadow of death, I will fear no evil, for you are with me; your rod and your staff, they comfort me'.

The assurance for comfort is of God.

The more I look at the power invested in a mother by God, the more I feel a sense of responsibility and accountability. It is clear that a mother can easily make or break the confidence of a child by their response. A mother's words can be so powerful that we have to remain prayerful and submitted under the guidance of the Holy Spirit to be able to move in this great assignment of comforting others that God has bestowed on us.

A mother needs to be so careful not to break the confidence of a child. Oftentimes a child may be discouraged or disappointed and needs a mother to inspire and comfort them to keep motivated. When a child is at a low point in what they are doing, they need a mother to be able to comfort them and tell them they can do it. It is powerful when a mother quietly finds out what the problem is and is able to bring a right word for the season. Oftentimes, a mother will have an idea without being told the problem and uniquely find the ideal words of comfort.

I would like to remind mothers that they have such great attributes to console. It is really such a comfort to know that you have someone to go to who will not judge you and say: 'what have you done and why have you done this?' but rather will embrace you with arms wide open. A mother is meant to bandage the wounds and wipe away the tears of their child by words that they utter. This helps the child find themselves again, be restored in the dream they were pursuing and know that they can be comforted again and again. Psalm 71:21 You will increase my greatness and comfort me again.

As mothers we too experience emotional pain and will also need support, yet the ability of a mother to be able to comfort is not of themselves. It is a divine ability by the power invested in us from on high. It is paramount that we take care of ourselves through intimacy with God, support from friends and the comforting words of God. Psalm 119:76: 'Let your steadfast love comfort me according to your promise to your servant'.

CHAPTER 4

A MOTHER OVERFLOWS
IN WISE COUNSEL

We now understand that there is an expectation on mothers to be able to function and give the best words of counsel.

Wise counsel is having the ability to give special advice to either a younger generation or someone less experienced in the field or situation, enabling them to make wiser decisions and avoid mistakes of the past. I believe that wise counsel produces a safety net for those receiving it; helping them to make fewer bad decisions. One bad decision can have consequential ripple effects that can affect not only the person making the decision, but can also negatively affect others connected to the decision-maker, for instance family, friends or business, and could impact many generations. Proverbs puts it this way 'Where there is no guidance, a people falls, but in an abundance of counsellors there is safety' *(Proverbs 11:14).*

In British Royalty, there is an interesting story of how a decision can affect a family's destiny from generation to generation; literally changing its course. Princess Elizabeth's grandfather, King George V, died in 1936. Her uncle became king after him, King Edward VIII. He became king only for a short time and decided to abdicate.

After he abdicated, his brother, Princess Elizabeth's father the Duke of York, became king, King George VI. This now put Princess Elizabeth in line to be Queen.

In 1951, the King's health was poor, he could not go to as many public events as he used to. Princess Elizabeth had to start making official visits for him. The King died on 6 February 1952. Princess Elizabeth was crowned queen on 2 June 1953 in Westminster Abbey. We can see that the decision of Queen Elizabeth's uncle to abdicate put her in line to be queen, and all her children and grandchildren are now part of the Royal Family.

The above is an example of how important our decisions are and why we need God's wisdom in application to every situation.

I am a great believer that wise counsel can only originate from the word of God. You may find helpful advice from other sources, i.e. books, websites or friends, but the best ideas stem from God in the first place, so the Holy Spirit will help us discern what is helpful and what is not. A mother needs to be completely reliant and dependent on God's word to be able to give the best counsel. This is because the word of God has a word for every situation in life. Proverbs 8:14 (KJV): 'counsel is mine, and sound wisdom: I am understanding; I have strength'. The more a mother abides in the word of God, the more wise the counsel and the more sound the judgment they can give. When God is allowed into a situation, He will take full pre-eminence in bringing to pass the word that he recommends. This is confirmed in Isaiah 55:11: 'So will My word be which goes forth from My mouth. It will not return to me empty, without accomplishing what I desire, and without succeeding in the matter for which I sent it'. So here we see that the counsel that is given based on the word of God is surely perfect. God will definitely watch over His word to perform it.

When someone takes on wise counsel, based on the word of God, the Holy Spirit then rests upon the person, giving them the ability to make the right decisions. This can be seen in Isaiah 11:2: 'And the Spirit of the Lord shall rest upon him, the Spirit of wisdom and understanding, the Spirit of counsel and might, the Spirit of knowledge and the fear of the Lord'. Remember, a relationship with God is the key – Proverbs 9:10: The fear of the Lord is the beginning of wisdom, and the knowledge of the Holy One is insight. The best is to get God's counsel in all situations. He is always ready and available to help us. The counsel of the Lord stands forever, the plans of His heart to all generations' *(Psalm 33:11)*.

As a mother offering wise counsel, remember to look after your own interests; always seeking counsel for yourself from the right sources. When we have a strong connection with God we can discern His wisdom more easily and hear Him speaking into the situations that we face. 'Blessed is the man who walks not in the counsel of the wicked, nor stands in the way of sinners, nor sits in the seat of scoffers; but his delight is in the law of the Lord, and on his law he meditates day and night' *(Psalm 1:1–2)*. Having the right people around will help you remain rooted in the word of God, thereby being steady in your faith and having the ability to stand the various winds of life that blow in your direction.

As a mother, no doubt you will find yourself in a place where your advice is not appreciated or is rejected. It is not obvious that your counsel will be valued. We have to realise that people are at different places in life and it might take a while to process the counsel. Some people might be influenced by peer pressure and might not have the strength to stand for something that's right. Others may have a lot of unprocessed emotional pain so they struggle to make good choices. My advice is to be able to softly share your wise counsel and give the person space to think about their decision. The Bible says in Proverbs 15:1: 'A soft answer turns away wrath, but a harsh word stirs up anger'. There is no benefit in forcing your counsel onto people. As mothers, we need to ensure that our decisions or words of counsel are exercised at the appropriate time in a well-managed environment. The context will affect how well the counsel can be received.

It can be really helpful to create a respectful environment for our children that will help the receiver to feel safe and accepted when hearing advice. Making sure we listen carefully to the receiver, truly hearing what they are saying and giving them space to talk uninterrupted will help them be more open to receive. When someone feels safe to seek advice, it can help encourage them to seek further wise counsel throughout their life.

I am a great believer that no matter the age, race, gender, generation or creed, all advice and counsel based on the word of God can never go out of fashion or be stale because there is life in the word.

Always remember that, as a mother, although you are regularly giving advice and wise counsel, there is need to increase in learning. I personally think it's tragic when I find a "know it all" mother. Proverbs 10:17: 'Whoever heeds instruction is on the path to life, but he who rejects reproof leads others astray'.

This simply means some are not open to ideas and can shut off hearing what's good for them, including the voice of God unfolding in their life. Always aspire to know and hear more that you may be able to give effective wise counsel. 'Let the wise hear and increase in learning, and the one who understands obtain guidance' *(Proverbs 1:5)*.

Once a mother figure establishes and embeds the essence of wise counsel in the recipient, it goes without saying that they are able to make wise choices which have a direct impact overall on their decision-making process and makes them literally stand out from the crowd. This is a great discipline that can be adopted, enhancing the success of many decisions made as they are made from a place of safety. It is important that a mother's dream for those they counsel is that they will be able to grow in godly wisdom by receiving the instructions and applying them in their own life without persuasion. They then are able to stand in total obedience to God.

Sometimes mother figures may take it for granted that the people they are offering wise counsel have understanding of the benefits of wise counsel. They may even get upset that they have done everything to help the person understand the wise counsel they keep giving and it's not appreciated. May I suggest the need to ensure there is adequate communication between the two parties so that the receiver has full understanding of the help at hand. It is important to help them realise that their decisions today will affect their tomorrow. How we respond in our current situation is what will determine who we are in the future. We need to respond wisely. Proverbs 16:25: 'There is a way that seems right to a man, but its end is the way to death'.

We can see that great godly counsel forms the foundation of good counselling and should help the receiver possess that which belongs to them as ordained by heaven. Proverbs 20:18: '[Every] purpose is established by counsel: and with good advice make war'.

A mother, giving advice to someone dependent on them for it, should realise the great responsibility upon them ensuring they give godly advice that creates safety.

Let all of us, therefore, that stands in the place of a mother, be able to apply ourselves well because the world needs our valuable counsel. They may not say it out loud, but they are crying out for this counsel in the many ways they are responding to situations and circumstances. I believe as a mother, you can use your position and the trust vested in you by God to make the world a better place by facilitating wise counsel in various ways. When a life is impacted in a positive way, I know that a community is also impacted. From there, a nation can be impacted too following on to the world effectively. The benefits of wise counsel create eternal rewards and blessings. 'For by wise guidance you can wage your war, and in abundance of counsellors there is victory' *(Proverbs 24:6)*. Let us therefore create and facilitate many opportunities for wise counsel. 'Without counsel plans fail, but with many advisers they succeed' *(Proverbs 15:22)*.

A mother's love, truly overflows in wise counsel that is bound to bring about worldwide transformation.

CHAPTER 5

A MOTHER IS COMPASSIONATE

Compassion is defined as the emotional response when perceiving suffering and involves an authentic desire to help. This can feel like concern for others. Oftentimes, a mother is the first person that comes to the mind of a child when they have a need that requires compassion. A mother is hardwired to ensure that their children's needs are met as best as they can be, and this is often a continuous task.

Research shows that our brains have the innate ability to perceive compassion, and we also have the capacity to grow in it. This is why we find that some feelings of compassion can come quite naturally, and others can develop as we grow as individuals. It is also why God has given us so many helpful reminders in The Bible on this subject. The Holy Spirit is so faithful in reminding us of things, both spiritual and practical. We have so much potential when we stay connected to Him, and He will prompt us in areas of need – both for ourselves and others.

Mother Teresa is one of the greatest examples in history of a compassionate woman. She was a mother to many known and unknown children, she is one of my heroes still today. Mother Teresa had a personality that affected everyone she came into contact with. She is widely known for her passionate, unselfish and brave charitable deeds. She was extremely hardworking and selfless in all her endeavours. She lived a life consecrated to Jesus, with joy and gladness of heart.

The key here is that she "lived a life consecrated to Jesus". Our fullest potential in motherhood does not come on its own. If we want to be compassionate and model compassion to others, we need to spend time with the one who has the ultimate compassionate heart – Jesus. I believe a mother's heart is designed to be compassionate, regardless of whether a 'child' is known or unknown.

It is amazing to find that, because this is how God intended us to function, when a mother shows compassion she experiences the satisfaction of being there for someone else, who as a result experiences joy and a sense of worth. This heart-warming exchange between a mother and a child or spiritual child encourages us to keep doing what we do. God is the great designer of humanity. When we stay close to Him, it becomes easier to flow in His will. In that place we can experience deep fulfilment and success, knowing that we are living in God's design. My own experience over the years has been that when I find out what I am created to do, I experience great delight in doing it. We don't always know what we are supposed to be doing, and that is ok; God will lead us step by step as we stay close to His heart.

I knew a lady who lost her job due to an illness that was very sudden. The woman could hardly cook or coordinate herself to look after her two-year-old son. So I decided to go out of my way by doing shopping for the family every week and making sure the boy was fed. They had no food so I took some ready meals for the family just to ease the burden they were going through. I can go on and on in giving you the various experiences I have had on this journey of showing compassion. It brings with it an unquestionable joy and fulfilment knowing that you have made a difference in someone's life.

Compassion is the most valuable form of care. It can be hard in today's culture to keep giving out to others when there are so many demands on our time and money. Yet God has enabled us to remain compassionate. I encourage every mother to ask for God's help in remaining compassionate according to Colossians 3:12: 'Put on then, as God's chosen ones, holy and beloved, compassionate hearts, kindness, humility, meekness, and patience'. God is faithful to impress on our hearts those who we have the capacity to help, and we will also find that our natural inclination towards compassion will grow as we go through our own experiences of need too.

The etymology of the word compassion comes from Latin meaning "to suffer with". A real mother feels with that person that looks up to them and has a dependency on them. A mother can feel the pain and anguish that the "child" feels, not only biological children but spiritual children or those whom God has placed in our heart to support. It really makes a difference when someone gives of themselves to walk through the suffering with the sufferer rather than just showing sympathy or acts of kindness. Mother Teresa was a great believer that being compassionate was a way of showing divine respect to the needy person.

So how can we suffer with those who are suffering? Here are just a few ideas:

Take time to simply listen, carefully. People don't want our judgements or comments on how they are feeling, they just want to feel heard. It can be so tempting to give advice or suggestions, but it is only respectful to do that if the person asks for it.

Stay in regular contact with someone who is hurting. A face to face conversation, message, phone call or email just saying: "I'm thinking of you" or "how are you doing today?" can make a big difference to somebody who is going through a trial that can make one feel isolated.

Can you remember a time when somebody supported you through a trial? What did they do for you and how did it make you feel?

I like to look at life from an angle where every person is where they are by the ultimate grace of God.

It is very important to be there for one another. We are reminded in Matthew 7:12 that: 'whatever you wish that others would do to you, do also to them, for this is the Law and the Prophets'. Compassion is so important because nobody chooses to be in a place of suffering and it can so easily happen to anyone; therefore, we need all the support we can get. We are designed to be there for each other according to Galatians 6:2: 'Bear one another's burdens, and so fulfil the law of Christ'. I must add that mothers should not feel compelled to do so but rather, this can be a process where mothers identify with the needs around them and start where they are. Praying about people who are in need of compassion is one way of showing compassion. The Holy Spirit will draw to our attention those who we have the capacity to help.

I believe a mother is in the position to show compassion by virtue of it being a gift from God. 'As each has received a gift, use it to serve one another, as good stewards of God's varied grace' *(1 Peter 4:10)*. I know that many people can give the gift of compassion, but I am specifically looking at the grace God has bestowed upon women in the area of love and compassion. The compassion that a mother is able to give is a result of God's divine ability and enablement.

I implore you by the mercy of God to be compassionate and kind hearted to everyone within your reach, according to your level of ability. I believe this is the path that the Lord Jesus Christ led for us. When Jesus walked on earth, he showed compassion to so many people. Ultimately, Jesus had compassion for you and me and that's why he paid the price by dying for us. I am not saying that we should die for anyone, but when we receive the deep compassion that the Father has for us, we are able to be compassionate more easily; 'I will show compassion to others, as my Saviour first showed compassion to me' *(1 John 4:19)*. We love, because He first loved us. There is every gain in standing in obedience to God's principles. So, it's not that I want you to show compassion but it's that this is a principle that works and is purely based on a personal decision to stand in obedience following God's direction. One thing I am certain of, is that God has never failed and He will never fail us. Neither has He ever lied and will never lie. The Bible declares: 'if anyone has the world's goods and sees his brother in need, yet closes his heart against him, how does God's love abide in him?' *(1 John 3:17)*. We therefore need to find it within our hearts to be able to show compassion as Gods love abides in us.

I understand that sometimes, it can be overwhelming to keep doing good for people. It can get to a point where the mother starts saying to herself, hang on, why do I have to do all this? Why only me? Why can't someone else do it? Remember to take care of yourself and ask for help when needed.

'Let us not grow weary of doing good, for in due season we will reap, if we do not give up' *(Galatians 6:9)*.

24

Whatever you do in secret, God will reward you. As you constantly show the labour of love in being there for children or those people looking up to you, you will effectively reap the rewards of heaven which are unstoppable. Therefore, when you do good for someone, don't look to them for a reward. Look to God.

When you look around, there are so many people in need of compassion. I believe our place as mothers is to do what we can for the people looking up to us or else they can be left feeling unwanted and helpless. See what Jesus did when he saw the needy. When he saw the crowds, he had compassion for them, because they were harassed and helpless: 'like sheep without a shepherd' *(Matthew 9:36)*.

Our needs will come in many different shapes or forms, and sometimes not in ways that we expect. The key is to be sensitive to the need of the hour and be able to help that most desperate need if we can. Zechariah 7:9: 'Thus says the Lord of hosts, Render true judgments, show kindness and mercy to one another. Being merciful and kind is an act of showing true compassion as God's children.' Each act of compassion that we choose makes a big difference to people's lives, and cumulatively makes the world a better place.

Compassion is an invaluable attribute as a mother. That deep love and ability to help change a situation is powerful. We are all on a journey with love. When we have our children, there is a natural, instinctive love that pours out of us from a place we didn't know existed. As our children grow, our love for them grows too. And as we stay connected with God, over time, our capacity to love has the potential to skyrocket.

I personally have found that when I show compassion to people it is a humbling experience that brings glory and honour to God, taking away focus from myself in a healthy way. We are encouraged to have a humble mind in 1 Peter 3:8: 'Finally, all of you, have unity of mind, sympathy, brotherly love, a tender heart, and a humble mind.'

Giving to the poor: Embracing God's children who are in need, God has asked us to always remember the poor. This is a way that we can extend our compassion as mothers to those of God's children who have needs that are different to our biological offspring. The poor hold a precious place in the heart of the father. Galatians 2:10: 'Only, they asked us to remember the poor, the very thing I was eager to do'. I know it can be challenging but we are encouraged by our saviour who was challenged, Hebrews 4:15: 'For we do not have a high priest who is unable to sympathize with our weaknesses, but one who in every respect has been tempted as we are, yet without sin.' God is not man that He should forget your labour of compassion. Whatever you do, God will repay you.

God has told us that when we remember the poor and are generous to them, we actually are lending to the Lord and God will repay us for all the compassion we are showing. 'Whoever is generous to the poor lends to the Lord, and he will repay him for his deed *(Proverbs 19:17)*.

Let's stand in the fear of God as we do His will; fulfilling righteousness *(Psalm 103:13)*.

As a father shows compassion to his children, so the Lord shows compassion to those who fear him. The fear of the Lord carries with it great discipline and tremendous benefits.

When compassion is challenging:

We will have various situations that will challenge our ability to be compassionate, yet we are encouraged to keep our focus on God for His continual guidance and leading at all times. Sometimes compassion may be so hard as your child or spiritual child may have done something very wrong towards you and then they find themselves in a desperate situation. They get to a point where they don't know where to run to. I am reminded of the story of the son who collected all his inheritance, went and spent it all and still came back to the father. The father did not judge him and so we are encouraged not to judge people but rather to embrace them and be available. Luke 15:20: 'And he arose and came to his father. But while he was still a long way off, his father saw him and felt compassion, and ran and embraced him and kissed him'.

We need to be a solution to the needy putting a smile upon their faces and not sit in the place of judgement. We are not responsible for people's happiness but we can certainly contribute to it. Every human being has flaws and we need to help each other keep our focus on attaining heaven by demonstrating it to others through our behaviour.

I personally visit a group of women in a refuge with a team of other women. We take gifts to them; covering the greatest need they have. I must say, the greatest constraint for me is time, but the joy and fulfilment that comes after visiting the refuge is amazing. The more I give of myself to the helpless and hopeless, the more God makes divine provision for me and my household in our area of need.

Let us keep our hearts connected to God, who enables us to have compassion on the child who needs it. Our greatest desire as human beings is for that unconditional, compassionate love that transforms us into His likeness. Let us model this to our kids who are always watching our example.

Luke 7:13: 'And when the Lord saw her, he had compassion on her'.

CHAPTER 6

A MOTHER ABIDES IN GOD'S PRESENCE

To abide in God is simply to choose Him as our dwelling. It is amazing to think that God, who is ultimate security, can actually be our place of residence. The psalmist puts it like this: 'O Lord, You have been our dwelling place in all generations' *(Psalm 90:1)*. This is an affirmation cry that generations before us have been dwelling in The Lord's presence for years and years. He identifies that the wanderers in the desert, whom he is addressing, have a permanent, consistent home in God, despite no physical house. Sometimes we can feel like wanderers as we try to navigate our way through motherhood – so many decisions to make, responsibilities to juggle and wounds from our own childhood to heal. As a mother, there is no better place to be than in God's presence. The essence of God is peace and assurance; so the more we abide in Him the more fulfilled we are as we realise that this is where the creator intended every woman to be. To "be" is the key here because first and foremost God created us as human beings, not human doings. We were created to know our place of rest in Him primarily before giving out through our work or caregiving. Everything flows from the place of intimacy in God's kingdom. And we execute our daily responsibilities so much better, with depth and excellence, when we are connected to the One who created our lives in the first place.

Dwelling in the presence of God brings wholeness and satisfaction. When we abide in God as mothers, we are able to get accurate instructions and direction for our lives from the Holy Spirit. He is so kind and considerate of the details in our lives. Abiding in the Holy Spirit brings mothers to a place of personal joy and gratitude to God.

The Lord Jesus encourages us in John 15:4–5 (New International Version): 'remain in me, as I also remain in you. No branch can bear fruit by itself; it must remain in the vine. Neither can you bear fruit unless you remain in me.

I am the vine; you are the branches. If you remain in me and I in you, you will bear much fruit; apart from me you can do nothing'.

Jesus exhorts us to remain in Him and promises that He will surely remain in us too. As mothers, we need to be connected right to the source in order to continue bearing the fruits of love, care, support and commitment. When we disconnect from the source, we dry out; unable to offer love and care as we have been created to. This can bring pain, disappointment and ungodly thoughts when we are not functioning in our ideal, God-given environment. In His presence we naturally give, as we give, we grow and we flourish.

When we remain in the Vine, we find ourselves being a blessing to many. 'If you remain in me and I in you, you will bear much fruit'.

My prayer is that every mother will not only dwell in God, but will abide all the days of our lives and continue to bring forth fruit that remains.

So how we can abide in God's presence as mothers?

This is achieved and enjoyed by having an intimate, special relationship with God; setting aside personal private time with God and inviting Him into aspects of our daily lives. Making the effort to actually set time apart with God, heart-to-heart, is often the best way to experience it. When you look at a couple in a relationship, there is a longing to spend quality time together which requires planning and effort for a level of intimacy to be achieved. This may mean finding a childminder, booking a restaurant or an activity to do together. And so it is with God. Of course we can speak to Him on the go, but if we want quality time it may mean scheduling it in when kids are asleep, getting childcare or planning a walk, for example.

When we have private time with God, it helps us to deepen in our desire for Him. A mother will also abide in God by regular immersion in the Word. Joshua 1:8 (English Standard Version) says: 'This Book of the Law shall not depart from your mouth, but you shall meditate on it day and night, so that you may be careful to do according to all that is written in it. For then you will make your way prosperous, and then you will have good success.'

This scripture confirms to me the fact that, when a mother recognises the essence of the word of God, desires it and obeys it, there is no way that heaven will not command a blessing in their lives. When a mother commits to love and care, they are living in obedience to God's word (whether they realise that or not) and as scripture is fulfilled, the blessing of the Lord is upon the mother.

A mother who pours out so much needs the word of God to get refreshing and renewed strength to keep loving people. When we read the word of God, and take time, not just to study but to meditate on it, it deepens our relationship with Jesus and increases our peace. A mother will need personal commitment to study and apply the instruction of God just like Ezra. Ezra 7:10 (ESV) says: 'For Ezra had set his heart to study the Law of the Lord, and to do it and to teach his statutes and rules in Israel'. What does this look like for you?

Mothers are always teaching, often by example, as they give out love and care. It is no wonder that we constantly become thirsty for more and more righteousness. We give out so much and our connection to the source of life is what enables and sustains us. A mother therefore needs to abide to function.

John 15:7 (ESV) says: 'If you abide in me, and my words abide in you, ask whatever you wish, and it will be done for you'.

Clearly scripture confirms that God delights in us abiding in him to the extent that He says He will give to us whatever we ask when we abide. From reading this, it affirms to me that it is no wonder the prayers of a crying mother never go unheard. A mother who pours herself out in Christ, abiding in Him, will always find joy and fulfilment in answered prayer and unexpected blessings.

This thirst turns into a deep desire for more and more of God. Matthew 5:6 (ESV) tell us: 'Blessed are those who hunger and thirst for righteousness, for they shall be satisfied'.

As we hunger and thirst for more righteousness, we can be filled to such a depth that over time we see that our nature is being replaced by God's. As a mother is operating from such a depth, she has a natural outpouring onto others of the love that she has been filled with.

My prayer is that every mother will recognise that they are such a special gift that is so unique and unmatched. When we dwell in God's presence, we hear more on the best course of action to take in our role as a mother. In other words, it is a safe place to be.

It is therefore very important that we take time to talk to God and hear from Him at all opportunities. As a mother takes time to abide in God, I say stay in the place of prayer, prayerfully and continually believing that the requests you bring before God, God will grant them continually. This is confirmed in the book of Mark 11:24: 'Therefore I tell you, whatever you ask in prayer, believe that you have received it, and it will be yours'.

As we have seen, when a mother stays in God's word, they are connected to the vine. As we remain connected to the source, there is a pathway that continues to flow through us; bringing life not just to us, but to people around us. As we are at one with God, we will continue to bear fruit. Good fruit that will last a lifetime. 'Fruit that displays the virtues of God: love, joy, peace, patience, kindness, goodness, faithfulness, gentleness, self-control; against such things there is no law' *(Galatians 5:22–23)*.

Sometimes life can be really hard, and a mother resorts to feeling tired of doing good. At these times, we need scriptures like the above to remind us to connect to the source, to hear what you need in that moment. Oftentimes we need to take a break too where possible, whatever that looks like for you. To have such a level of virtues and characteristics, it will take a closer walk with Jesus, abiding at his footstool daily. Just as a child usually runs to see their parent(s) first thing in the morning, sees them last thing at night and often communes with them during the day, so are we to be with God; knowing our need for Him all day long.

As we abide, we see great fruit and one of the greatest I have experienced is the gift of love. With the gift of love, A mother's face is always a child's glory. It is wonderful to have a steadfast mother who is doing her best to love according to God's word. 1 Peter 4:8 says: 'above all, keep loving one another earnestly, since love covers a multitude of sins'. Sometimes, mothers end up in tears because they have done something really nice or even lived for their children but the children don't seem to appreciate them. Yet God reminds us that perfect love casts out all fear and the more you keep loving the children, the less you are actually affected by what could really make a mother upset. A mother's love, a mother's heart is so unique. A mother is encouraged in 1 Peter 1:22 (ESV): 'having purified your souls by your obedience to the truth for a sincere brotherly love, love one another earnestly from a pure heart'. A mother loves people in total obedience to God as we are encouraged to love one another from a pure heart. A mother's love is so unique and selfless bringing with it a genuine restoration to those that are embraced. The love, care and support a mother gives is natural and she does not require payment for it. Hence, my advice to a mother is, don't grow weary in doing good, for in due time, you will reap the rewards of your labour of love.

'And it is my prayer that your love may abound more and more, with knowledge and all discernment' *(Philippians 1:9 ESV)*.

It is important for a mother to have wisdom, knowledge and discernment on how to give of their love so that they can make the right decisions at the right time and also not get burned out by doing too much. Moreover, a mother needs to be sensitive to the needs of the people they are offering love and care to, ensuring it is really what the other person wants. 'Let all that you do be done in love' *(1 Corinthians 16:14)*. If it's not wanted, it's not loving.

As a mother abides in God, they reach a point of seeing things from God's perspective. So, it is no longer about their effort, but it is about God and them in partnership. In such cases, we are filled with what I would call a Godly passion to love and to care for our children or people looking up to us. We get to a point where our hearts cry is to love people. A mother at this point is not looking for any payback or reward for their labour of love, but is simply there to offer authentic love and care to a child. They do everything to get the child to a place of freedom, joy and fulfilment. A mother therefore realises that the most important thing is really to commit to pray for all the loved ones looking up to them, and submit to God's word.

A mother's love, a mother's heart remains restless when salvation is missing. A mother treasures the day when a child makes a commitment to accept Jesus Christ as Lord and saviour. Salvation for children around her, regardless of whether they are biological or not brings great joy and delight. A mother's love embraces the gift of salvation. We need to continually seek and desire that the people looking up to us, can actually seek the uniqueness that lies inside of us. The uniqueness of a mother's love, a mother's heart is truly an inspiration from the connection we have with our God. As mothers, there is need to help those looking unto us who desire salvation. The ability of a mother to help those looking up to them to be saved, and remain in God is a special treasure that requires that we abide in God.

CHAPTER 7

A MOTHER'S HEART BUILDS UNITY

'How good and pleasant it is when brothers dwell together in unity! It is like the precious oil on the head, running down on the beard, on the beard of Aaron, running down on the collar of his robes! It is like the dew of Hermon, which falls on the mountains of Zion! For there the Lord has commanded the blessing, life forevermore' *(Psalm 133:1–3)*.

What a promise! Life is found in unity. When we dwell together in the oneness of seeking God together, we experience the anointing of the Holy Spirit – who is life itself. The precious anointing oil referenced in this verse alludes to Exodus 30:22–33: a holy oil blended with four spices: myrrh, cinnamon, cassia and cane. The mixture of these very different spices represents our need for each other. God could have just chosen one ingredient, but it was the blend of spices that made the oil holy. This is a wonderful image of our need for each other to make us holy. A beautiful fragrance is released when we, with all our differences, dwell together in oneness. A fragrance that can spread to many places. Just as the oil was poured on the priest Aaron's head, yet ran down to the hem of his robe. When we dwell together in unity, the effects are far reaching.

Establishing an environment of unity is so important because we have a significant influence on our children, our community and therefore society. In a world that can be increasingly self-centred, unity is paramount. Paul says in Philippians 2:3: 'do nothing out of selfish ambition or vain conceit. Rather, in humility value others above yourselves'. Mother figures are in a unique position where, through the choices we make, we can create unity or discord.

A mother is frequently thinking of how she can bring a solution and resolve matters to result in peace and stability. As mothers we are a source of empowerment to people around us; enabling them to be what God has called them to be. A mother operates from a spirit of humility, having power under control and not making anyone feel lesser than they are. When we look at Jesus, our role model, all He did was in care and sacrifice for us, to the extent of laying down His own life. He asks us to love in the same way.

Connection breeds unity

When we're united with God we want unity with people. Mothers often get tired and need to rest, yet we gain continual refreshment by staying in God. As we continually feed our spirit, we have the extraordinary ability and strength to deal with whatever life throws at us; desiring unity through it. It is only by God given ability that mothers can persevere against all odds and maintain an atmosphere of oneness amongst loved ones.

As we promote unity, a secure foundation is built in the lives of our children and the people looking up to us. The more unity is fostered by a mother, the greater the family bonds and consequently the greater the wider benefits.

There is such blessing and fulfilment as a mother in seeing how lives can be transformed by a heart of unity. Unity promotes oneness and wholeness and as such, harmony is established. Have you noticed how your child, people looking up to you or congregation exudes contentment when they are being nurtured by a heart of unity? When they know that you and God are for them and not against them? *(Romans 8:31)*.

Unity is essential in the life of every human being. Families and communities achieve very little if the desire for unity is absent. A mother is catalytic in this. We can achieve so much when living in unison with family or friends compared to living in isolation. It is essential for us to realise that unity is an attitude that can be chosen at all times. When a mother's heart is so postured in unconditional love, great untold benefits are seen and experienced. A mother has the golden privilege to ensure there are no divisions among the people and communities as encouraged in 1 Corinthians 1:10 (ESV): 'I appeal to you, brothers, by the name of our Lord Jesus Christ, that all of you agree, and that there be no divisions among you, but that you be united in the same mind and the same judgment'.

Promoting unity does not mean that the people will agree on everything. It is good to bear with each other and understand that we can see things differently. Sometimes, it may just be that you are both looking at the same outcome but your approach is different. A great example is that of a husband and wife. The husband and wife are uniquely different to one another and certainly don't always share the same opinions but they have a common foundation they are building on - unity. They stand together, and for each other, desiring oneness above being 'right'.

It is often helpful is to remember that we are all doing our best. Most of us, most of the time, are doing the best that we can based on where we are at in life and in God. 'Love believes all things [looking for the best in each one]' *(1 Corinthians 13:7 AMP)*. It's so affirming to know that God focuses on the best things in us, and this helps us to love ourselves better. When we see ourselves in this way we begin to want to draw out the best in others too. In line with this, it is necessary to have clear boundaries with those looking up to you. Boundaries are there to help us and others to be our best. We each have our own values and levels of time and energy, so it is important to be honest with ourselves and others about what capacity we have. God can increase our capacity as we grow, but it's essential to stay in tune with Him to know how to best use our energy in each season.

Prayer Unifies

Prayer unifies us, whether we're together or apart. Prayerfully bringing requests before heaven on behalf of the people that look up to us helps us grow closer to each other. I believe as a mother, it is essential to ensure prayer is paramount in everything that we do. Prayer helps us gain God's heart for the person in front of us; seeing them the way He does. Prayer also helps us gain God's heart for the congregation as a whole. The more we pray for the group we have been entrusted with, the more we see the heavenly purposes of it here on earth.

Likewise, as we pray communally, our bond is strengthened and our unity is affirmed.

The building of unity by a mother is only possible because of the intimacy she has with God. When a mother stays in the presence of God, they overflow in love that enables them to make decisions in unity. The Bible puts it this way: 'above all these put on love, which binds everything together in perfect harmony' *(Colossians 3:14 ESV).*

Equality through differences

As mothers, we are called to love everyone, not just those who are good to us. 'But I say to you who hear, Love your enemies, do good to those who hate you, bless those who curse you, pray for those who abuse you' *(Luke 6:27-28).*

When we are so united, we will make the world wonder at our love and unity causing great impact and will desire to know our Lord and Saviour Jesus Christ.

As Christians, lead by example and do everything to remain united as good examples. We need to get to a point where the mother's love, the mother's heart draws those looking up to them together. A mother stands in the unique position of ensuring that there are no divisions in the Christian life. Paul shows us an example of how he urges Christians to ensure they live in unity in 1 Cor. 1:10: 'I appeal to you, brothers, in the name of our Lord Jesus Christ, that all of you agree with one another so that there may be no divisions among you and that you may be perfectly united in mind and thought'. This shows that the divisions within children or families is nothing new, but we need to work at it and that's why I believe mothers, can make a great difference. A mother, always makes influence upon the people that surround her but a Spirit Filled Mother is of even greater influence.

We have people from different walks of life walking through the church doors. Sometimes, people are newly saved and they walk into the church still struggling with sin. We all have our weaknesses. It is my prayer that when we walk through the door, we will not judge anyone but will make them feel welcome as they are. A mother can encourage those looking up to them or the people around in their area of calling. When there is unity, every person does what they should be doing and together purposes are established. For instance, the human body has many members, for example the eye, legs, hands, mouth etc and none of these are beneficial on their own but it is only when they are all working together in unity that we see achievement. 'For as in one body we have many members, and the members do not all have the same function, so we, though many, are one body in Christ, and individually members one of another' *(Romans 12:4-5)*.

A mother is pivotal in changing the atmosphere around her and if we take our rightful position in God, I am sure that the world will be a better place.

So then let us pursue what makes for peace and for mutual upbuilding *(Romans 14:19)*.

A mother's love, a mother's heart is built on a solid foundation of unity doing away with gossip, slander or any negativity. A mother's love, a mother's heart's advice is not based on personal preferences and opinions but rather is centred on God. A mother therefore has a duty to ensure a positive impact to the people God has entrusted in her care. This is of paramount importance if we are to accomplish God's purpose. To stay in a place of humility as a mother is so rewarding and creates harmony.

Romans 12:16 (ESV) says: 'Live in harmony with one another. Do not be haughty, but associate with the lowly. Never be wise in your own sight'.

My prayer for all mothers is in accordance to Paul's letter to the Romans.

Romans 15:5-7 (ESV): 'May the God of endurance and encouragement grant you to live in such harmony with one another, in accord with Christ Jesus, that together you may with one voice glorify the God and Father of our Lord Jesus Christ. Therefore welcome one another as Christ has welcomed you, for the glory of God.

This will be a great achievement, when a mother's love, a mother's heart acknowledges the essence of our salvation and establishes accurate goals such as remembering the poor, the needy, the orphans and above all, not neglecting the assembling together as Christians. However, this is only attainable through the unity of the

Spirit in the bond of peace. Paul puts it this way in his letter to the Ephesians.

Ephesians 4:1-3 (KJV):

> '[1]I therefore, the prisoner of the Lord, beseech you that ye walk worthy of the vocation wherewith ye are called,
> [2]With all lowliness and meekness, with longsuffering, forbearing one another in love;
> [3]Endeavouring to keep the unity of the Spirit in the bond of peace'. ...

My plea to every mother is to realise how much God has entrusted us and to desire to please our master. A mother stands at that trusted position where she has children and people looking up to her as a mother. We need to recognise how much God has bestowed on us and to live a life worthy of our calling in the mighty name of our Lord Jesus Christ.

1 Peter 3:8 (ESV): Finally, all of you, have unity of mind, sympathy, brotherly love, a tender heart, and a humble mind.

Colossians 3:15-17 (ESV): 'And let the peace of Christ rule in your hearts, to which indeed you were called in one body. And be thankful. Let the word of Christ dwell in you richly, teaching and admonishing one another in all wisdom, singing psalms and hymns and spiritual songs, with thankfulness in your hearts to God. And whatever you do, in word or deed, do everything in the name of the Lord Jesus, giving thanks to God the Father through him'.

CHAPTER 8

A MOTHER IS FORGIVING

As humans, we all get hurt or offended. Mothers are in a position where we will often encounter conflict with our children, loved ones, people looking up to us or congregation. Yet it's not always that easy to forgive. Life can be painful and sometimes we can't see a way through the situation. I believe that God, who has created a mother so intuitively, is able to give the ability to do what may seem impossible. Philippians 4:13 (KJV): 'I can do all things through Christ who strengthens me'. This doesn't mean stifle your feelings. God is not ashamed of our feelings – we can express them to Him (or a trusted friend) and He will empower us to move forward in love. I believe there is a special grace on mothers to look at the circumstances at hand and find it within ourselves to hear God's instruction and direction concerning the matter. A mother can have such a positive impact in many lives as we are in a unique position where we are trusted and relied on. That's why practicing forgiveness regularly is so influential – we are literally demonstrating the unconditional love of God to our families; showing them they will not be rejected if they mess up. Our children can learn from a young age what healthy relationship looks like, and our congregation and those looking up to us can gain a healthy perspective on relationships where they perhaps haven't had one before. As mothers, we can take the lead in how we respond which can bring about peace, harmony and resolution in our lives and those around us.

The world we live in is such that everyone makes mistakes. A lot of times, you find judgement being made on the people who have made mistakes. The Bible is very clear to us on how to respond in such situations which we will explore. It is very important to recognise that we all need forgiveness. I believe mothers are so influential that through forgiveness we can impact the world around us. God has set us an example of forgiveness and we need to be able to forgive. If we do not forgive, God will not forgive us too. I am reminded of the fact that Jesus our Lord and Saviour was innocent yet: 'He was bruised for our iniquities; the chastisement of our peace was laid upon Him' *(Isaiah 53:5 ESV)*.

'But he was wounded for our transgressions; he was crushed for our iniquities; upon him was the chastisement that brought us peace, and with his stripes we are healed.'

So, the above is the greatest, most profound and highest example of forgiveness. Jesus was hung on the cross and condemned to death by accusers who plotted against his life to accuse him and condemn him to death. This is the highest form of allegation that I have come across, yet Christ still forgave them. He said in Luke 23:34: 'Father, forgive them for they know not what they are doing'. If we could get to this level of forgiveness, I am sure that this world will be a better place. I say this because mothers are so influential, respected and often, the most consulted in families.

Remember, Jesus knew no sin and is the Son of God, yet was willing to forgive.

When Jesus was being hung on the cross, his accusers were not sorry but rather mocked and jeered Him. They mocked him saying: 'If you are the King of Israel, come down from the cross and save yourself'. The passers-by hurled insults at Jesus yet He did not count this worthy of holding a grudge against His accusers. My prayer is that every mother can reflect on Jesus experience to identify a true heart of forgiveness and consequently emulate Christ. When a mother lays this foundation of forgiveness, it is without doubt that she will be an example to those looking up to her and they will be guided accordingly. As such, our loved ones will learn what forgiveness looks like and develop their own heart of forgiveness.

The Bible says:

'For if you forgive men when they sin against you, your heavenly Father will also forgive you. But if you do not forgive men their sins, your Father will not forgive your sins' *(Matthew 6:14–15)*. Jesus is talking temporally here, not eternally. He is driving home the point that our sins after faith can still hold earthly consequences. When we hold on to unforgiveness it inhibits our communion with God. The Lord will forgive us from the earthly consequences of our sins provided we are willing to show forgiveness to others (which is a part of our mission to show the love of Christ to the world).

It can be so hard to forgive someone who has genuinely done something that has caused you a lot of pain. I want to encourage you to walk through the process with God a step at a time. Verses like these do not negate the need to process pain with a trusted friend, counsellor or God Himself. But I know The Bible tells me: 'to forgive 70 times seven' *(Matthew 18:21-22)*, which means it is a necessity integral to our Christian walk.

'21Then came Peter to him, and said, "Lord, how often shall my brother sin against me, and I forgive him? till seven times?"
22Jesus saith unto him, "I say not unto thee, Until seven times: but, Until seventy times seven".'

It is astounding how much stagnation comes with unforgiveness. Holding onto grudges and bitterness can delay opportunities in our lives, cause physical illnesses or pain.

Forgiveness is clearly very necessary for our wellbeing and is not to be taken lightly.

So, no matter how much a mother may be wronged, it makes a big difference to be quick to forgive and consequently encourage the same to people who go to us with issues of unforgiveness.

Ephesians 4:32 says: 'Be kind and compassionate to one another, forgiving each other, just as in Christ God forgave you'.

It is important for us as mothers to create an atmosphere where people feel safe to make mistakes and to learn to bear with one another. To bring understanding that there is no need to hold on to bitterness, grief, strife, rage and anger… but rather to embrace forgiveness. The Bible confirms this to us in Colossians 3:13: 'Bear with each other and forgive whatever grievances you may have against one another. Forgive as the Lord forgave you'. Romans 12:18 (ESV): 'If possible, so far as it depends on you, live peaceably with all'.

It is important to remember that no one is perfect and that we all make mistakes. Ecclesiastes 7:20 says: 'Not a single person on earth is always good and never sins'. We are all imperfect. A mother needs to encourage people around her to be quick to forgive and not to dwell on the matter that has upset them, as it is likely that continuously thinking about what upset them would lead to more anger to a point of grudge and unforgiveness resulting in more negative responses and outcomes. I believe it's better for a mother to make the decision to respond to evil with good as love covers a multitude of sins. A mother is in a position to make the person who is hurt refocus and feel light-hearted concerning the matter and embrace forgiveness. Support will have to be provided in explaining the need of not dwelling on who hurt them and why they were hurt, but rather to understand that the offenders actions are based on a lack of understanding of love in God. Offence is such a terrible thing that the longer the offended dwells on a matter, the harder it becomes to confess and in turn the offended is going to suffer many more losses in their own personal life.

It is important to focus on God's purpose for your life, which is greater than any problem or pain you might be currently facing in the area of unforgiveness. This is a hard statement but it's a fact. When we learn to love one another genuinely from the heart, we will pay little attention to the few times when we may be wronged. We will learn to love regardless and believe me, we will forego many heartaches from brothers and sisters. Peter confirms this by saying: 'Above all, love each other deeply, because love covers over a multitude of sins'. I Peter 4:8: It is of great necessity to acknowledge that love is the most important attribute we can show to one another.

So now faith, hope, and love abide, these three; but the greatest of these is love.

The famous "love chapter" in 1 Corinthians 13 says: 'love keeps no record of wrongs' *(1 Corinthians 13:5 New International Version (NIV)* in quote:

> '5It does not dishonour others, it is not self-seeking, it is not easily angered, it keeps no record of wrongs.'

There are people who have deep wounds or have experienced trauma that causes big distress. It is important to take time to listen to the person and to give the person space to express how they feel. Forgiveness doesn't always come about immediately but may be something that has to be worked on over time and then healing comes. Depending on the issue and how the Lord leads, it may be helpful to suggest therapy to some.

I have had situations where someone confesses that they have done something really bad and they don't see a way out. They may take the opportunity of confiding in a mother or mother figure that they trust. I believe in situations such as this, It's important to help the person realise that the Lord will forgive them and also to walk through the journey of forgiveness with them, establishing the right course of action to follow as confirmed in the scripture above.

The key is to remember that forgiveness is essentially a matter of the heart. It is not just what we do or what we say because it is possible to show acts of kindness but be bitter on the inside. It is important to establish what forgiveness actually is because sometimes we can think we have forgiven by saying kind words but the grudge still sits heavily within our heart. As we look inward, forgiveness will come from the heart and follow on with good words and acts of kindness.

Forgiveness is essentially how we work through pain or offence with God. Forgiveness is greatly based on the relationship between the person who is offended and God. God is very clear about the issue of forgiveness. God has set a standard for us all in Mark 11:25 (ESV): 'whenever you stand praying, forgive, if you have anything against anyone, so that your Father also who is in heaven may forgive you your trespasses'. We cannot carry on as usual if there is unforgiveness lingering over our heads, we need to forgive and let go that our Heavenly Father may forgive us too.

Let all bitterness and wrath and anger and clamor and slander be put away from you, along with all malice. 'Be kind to one another, tenderhearted, forgiving one another, as God in Christ forgave you' *(Ephesians 4:31-32 ESV)*.

Many times I have been hurt by people, but I have trained and re-trained myself each time to forgive. Forgiveness is essentially a choice and a decision that one can make to release people from the offences against you. I understand that pain will be there, the memories of the hurt may be deep, but we can be released from the bondage of feeling stuck in it through forgiveness.

We can make the choice to forgive even when the other person doesn't want to forgive or be reconciled. Wisdom needs to be applied because as you forgive, you need to be mindful not to put yourself in the same vulnerable situation. God will speak to you and guide you in this as you seek Him.

When Peter asked Jesus how many times we should forgive someone who has sinned against us, Jesus answered him in Matthew 18:21-22 (ESV): 'Then Peter came up and said to him, "Lord, how often will my brother sin against me, and I forgive him? As many as seven times?" Jesus said to him, "I do not say to you seven times, but seventy times seven'. If you do the maths, that's about 490 times. To me, this is a staggering amount of sin, a staggering amount of pain and a staggering amount of forgiveness. Basically, my interpretation of this is, forgive countless times, because no one can comprehend writing down each time they are offended and each time they forgive.

Unprocessed anger, frustration, malice, grudges, bitterness are subtle tormentors that cause changes in heart rate, blood pressure and immune response. Those changes, then, increase the risk of depression, heart disease and diabetes, among other conditions. Forgiveness, however, calms stress levels, leading to improved health. I call them tormentors because they make you stop functioning in your usual way and cause you wasted days of endless negative thoughts that are not profitable in any way, shape or form. They cause you bitterness of heart and sadness. All the joy is robbed and by this, I always imagine that there is only one winner, the devil, the liar, the accuser of the brethren. All this can be avoided and you can free yourself by forgiving regularly and letting go. I am reminded of the unforgiving servant who was forgiven but would not forgive his colleague in Matthew 18:21-35 (ESV):

'21Then Peter came up and said to him, "Lord, how often will my brother sin against me, and I forgive him? As many as seven times?"

22Jesus said to him, "I do not say to you seven times, but seventy-seven times".

23Therefore the kingdom of heaven may be compared to a king who wished to settle accounts with his servants.

[a] 24When he began to settle, one was brought to him who owed him ten thousand talents.

[b]25And since he could not pay, his master ordered him to be sold, with his wife and children and all that he had, and payment to be made.

26So the servant[c] fell on his knees, imploring him, "Have patience with me, and I will pay you everything."

27And out of pity for him, the master of that servant released him and forgave him the debt.

28But when that same servant went out, he found one of his fellow servants who owed him a hundred denarii,[d] and seizing him, he began to choke him, saying, "Pay what you owe".

29So his fellow servant fell down and pleaded with him, "Have patience with me, and I will pay you."

30He refused and went and put him in prison until he should pay the debt.

31When his fellow servants saw what had taken place, they were greatly distressed, and they went and reported to their master all that had taken place.

32Then his master summoned him and said to him, "You wicked servant! I forgave you all that debt because you pleaded with me.

33And should not you have had mercy on your fellow servant, as I had mercy on you?"

34And in anger his master delivered him to the jailers,[e] until he should pay all his debt.

35So also my heavenly Father will do to every one of you, if you do not forgive your brother from your heart".'

Dear brothers and sisters, let's forgive from the heart and let go, it is so worth it. We all go before God and have sins piled up so high, He has forgiven us yet we refuse to forgive. Let's not torment ourselves by refusing to forgive and giving the enemy a free course in our lives. Let's remember, we are all human and that no one is perfect. Let's forgive without waiting for the person who has offended us to make the first approach. Let's be ready to let go and let God. There is need to let go of bitterness and unforgiveness and all hard feelings. God is the true judge who will fight for you if only you let Him. He has told us to pray for our enemies and to do good to those who despitefully use us or persecute us.

Luke 6:27–28 (ESV): 'But I say to you who hear, Love your enemies, do good to those who hate you, bless those who curse you, pray for those who abuse you.'

The miracle of forgiveness will come easy to the one who is ready for it. Forgiveness is therefore not an option for a Christian if we say we want to follow Christ. The miracle we have received from God of forgiveness of sins is what God expects us to give to others too. Be willing to forgive, just as Jesus willingly forgave us. If you want to be set free, you need to forgive. You can never be set free until you forgive. Let's lay aside the sin that does so easily beset us. We need to do everything as Christlike not to willingly get ourselves stained with sin and remember that we are actually washed by the precious blood of our Lord and saviour Jesus Christ. Whenever we are gripped with unforgiveness, let's remember to run to the cross and we will surely be saved, helped and washed clean. To understand what total forgiveness is all about, you need to trust Jesus Christ as your personal Lord and Saviour.

In conclusion to this chapter, I would now like to encourage every mother and every woman to remember this: Colossians 3:8–13 (ESV):

'8But now you must put them all away: anger, wrath, malice, slander, and obscene talk from your mouth.
9Do not lie to one another, seeing that you have put off the old self[a] with its practices

[10]and have put on the new self, which is being renewed in knowledge after the image of its creator.

[11]Here there is not Greek and Jew, circumcised and uncircumcised, barbarian, Scythian, slave,[b] free; but Christ is all, and in all.

[12]Put on then, as God's chosen ones, holy and beloved, compassionate hearts, kindness, humility, meekness, and patience,

[13]bearing with one another and, if one has a complaint against another, forgiving each other; as the Lord has forgiven you, so you also must forgive.'

Further verses on Forgiveness

I would like to remind every person that when God is obeyed, everything else falls into place, yes, including enemies.

Proverbs 16:7 (ESV): 'When a man's ways please the Lord, he makes even his enemies to be at peace with him'.

2 Corinthians 13:11 (ESV): 'Finally, brothers, rejoice. Aim for restoration, comfort one another, agree with one another, live in peace; and the God of love and peace will be with you'.

If we love God truly, we will keep his commandments. This is confirmed in John 14:15 (ESV): 'If you love me, you will keep my commandment'.

When we keep Gods commandments, we will be able to please Him easily.

Romans 12:20-21 (ESV): "if your enemy is hungry, feed him; if he is thirsty, give him something to drink; for by so doing you will heap burning coals on his head. Do not be overcome by evil, but overcome evil with good."

CHAPTER 9

THE ULTIMATE IN A MOTHER'S LOVE IS THE FEAR OF GOD

Some of us may struggle with fearing God if we were raised by a parent who was harsh with us and instilled unhealthy fear in us. This is something God understands and He will help you with it as you surrender your life to Him. The more we study the character of God the more we will learn about His loving nature and be able to separate healthy respect from unhealthy fear. There is an old saying: respect is earned, not given; this reminds me of the verse: 'we love because He first loved us' *(1 John 4:19)*. We learn respect from God Himself – He has given us the dignity to choose Him through Jesus, He does not force Himself on us in arrogance; it's His love that compels us. The following verse affirms the purity and holiness of God's character, a character that is completely opposed with the harsh, prideful treatment you may have encountered:

'The fear of the Lord is hatred of evil. Pride and arrogance and the way of evil and perverted speech I hate' *(Proverbs 8:13 ESV)*.

The above scripture shows us the sovereignty of our Lord. I encourage all mothers to model respect based on a healthy fear of a Holy God. Why do I believe this is so important? The Bible says in Proverbs 16:6 (ESV): 'By steadfast love and faithfulness iniquity is atoned for, and by the fear of the Lord one turns away from evil.' In order to have the ability to give Godly counsel mothers need this reverential fear of God. When God is at the centre of decision making, purposes are established in the will of God. We all can reckon with the fact a mother's counsel is one of the highest counsels sought after without putting much thought to it. Hence my desire that every woman will understand that knowledge and respond practically. I am very optimistic that when mothers are in right standing with God, then they will give such wise counsel based on God's word and the Holy Spirit.

The psalmist instructs us to honour God in Psalm 33:8, 'Let all the earth fear the Lord; let all the inhabitants of the world stand in awe of Him'.

When a mother fears God, she adores Him and does her best not to upset Him. Part of not offending God and staying in reverential fear of God is when giving wise Godly counsel. The most Important aspect we need to remember is that the fear of God is the beginning of knowledge and understanding. It is the beginning of wisdom. This is confirmed in Proverbs 1:7 (ESV): 'The fear of the Lord is the beginning of knowledge; fools despise wisdom and instruction'. Why? Because God knows what is best for us, so when we put him first we get to see His wisdom and walk in it. Sometimes that may be through the Holy Spirit; we might get an impression, word or picture, or it may be through reading The Bible. The Bible is full of guidance and direction for instance, one of the most common causes of disputes is unforgiveness. A mother full of wise counsel will follow the revealed word of God by giving guidance using for instance the following scriptures Matthew 6:14–15 (ESV):

'For if you forgive others their trespasses, your heavenly Father will also forgive you, but if you do not forgive others their trespasses, neither will your Father forgive your trespasses'.

And also Ephesians 4:32 (ESV) Which says: 'Be kind to one another, tenderhearted, forgiving one another, as God in Christ forgave you'.

The Bible is therefore clear on how to deal with unforgiveness based on the above scriptures and many more. Hence, it is why I believe mothers need so much of the fear of God for us to have godly counsel. And the psalmist puts it this way in Psalm 111:10 (ESV): 'The fear of the Lord is the beginning of wisdom; all those who practice it have a good understanding. His praise endures forever!'

If we deny the fear of God, we cut ourselves from the only source of wisdom. I implore mothers not to deceive ourselves thinking we have our own wisdom but to realise that wisdom comes from the fear of the Lord. We need to step back and let God lead us by consciously making the effort give every aspect of our lives to Him.

As we practice the fear of God, there is such great understanding that comes with it. Proverbs 9:10 (ESV): 'The fear of the Lord is the beginning of wisdom, and the knowledge of the Holy One is insight'. The mother in her quest to practice the fear of God, will naturally operate in God given wisdom. We need to continually ask God for His guidance and leading. When we ask, God always grants us our hearts desire.

The Bible also tells us in Matthew 5:6 (ESV):

'Blessed are those who hunger and thirst for righteousness, for they shall be satisfied'. In our hungering and thirsting after righteousness God promises to direct our paths; enabling us to show others the right way too. A mother, is a very key person that if she gets it right, many blessings will be bestowed upon her, her household and everyone looking up to her. When mothers get to this position, they will be more inclined to please their master. The psalmist says in Psalm 86:11: 'Teach me your way, O Lord, that I may walk in your truth; unite my heart to fear your name'.

When a mother has a steadfast, undivided heart, she holds God most reverent in her life and will make decisions that are God inspired. A decision that is God inspired will always carry with it an aroma of peace, joy and harmony. Such a mother's drive will not be based on personal gain or gratification but rather her biggest heart's desire will be to please her heavenly Father. The children and people looking up to the mother will get Godly understanding because of knowledge of the Holy one. When we hold onto God in reverential fear, the pureness of our heart increases because we experience the pleasure of our Father over us, like a child.

The Bible says in Psalm 19:9: 'the fear of the Lord is clean, enduring forever; the rules[a] of the Lord are true and righteous altogether.'

We need to understand that the "fear of God" does not mean to be afraid of God.

2 Timothy 1:7 (KJV) clarifies this by saying: 'For God hath not given us the spirit of fear; but of power, and of love, and of a sound mind.' It is rather important to understand God's nature. We need to revere Him for who He is. He is our king of kings, the

Lord of Lords, the all-knowing father, the magnificence creator, the commander of the heavenly battalion, the bright morning star, the root and the offspring of David, the I Am who says I AM. Proverbs 8:13 (ESV):

'The fear of the Lord is hatred of evil. Pride and arrogance and the way of evil and perverted speech I hate'.

Hence, if we say we fear God, it needs to be clear that we hate evil. God is our almighty God clothed in splendour and honour. We are reminded by Paul in Titus to steer away from ungodliness: 'They profess to know God, but they deny him by their works. They are detestable, disobedient, unfit for any good work' *(Titus 1:16 ESV)*. My Prayer is that as mothers, we will hold ourselves accountable to God, as well as knowing His grace. My prayer is that we will let our yes be yes and no be no, that we shall not be found in a wavering situation where we are standing in a compromising position. We need to embrace the disciplines of the fear of God and respect God in all we do; in awe of who He is. Philippians 2:12-13 (ESV): 'Therefore, my beloved, as you have always obeyed, so now, not only as in my presence but much more in my absence, work out your own salvation with fear and trembling, for it is God who works in you, both to will and to work for his good pleasure'.

Mothers ought to guide those looking up to them that they need to offer continuous reverential fear of God at all times regardless of the situation or the circumstances. Mothers need to do what is right and guide those looking up to them rightly, not because there is an audience but rather because they hold God in high esteem at all times. Hence to advise accordingly based on God's word for every situation they find themselves sorting out. Mothers will need to realise that God is the solution wherever they find themselves and despite the circumstance. It would also be wise as a mother to talk to God before giving your opinion and counsel, this could be as easy as a short inward prayer saying, Lord help me to give wise counsel, am relying on you.

Mothers find themselves in the unique position of making several decisions whether in their families, children or people looking up to them. It is important for mothers to emphasise the reverence of God, as being dishonest carries with it many consequences some of which may not be seen straight away but they will surely follow. Hebrews 12:29 reminds us that: 'for our God is a consuming fire'.

Mothers need to instil enough discipline in their children to the point they personally can identify that God is a consuming Fire. Though life may seem really hard, it is important to recognise that the fear of God enables us to get through what may seem to be very challenging times. God always answers our prayers when we put Him first. Psalm 145:19 states: 'He fulfils the desire of those who fear him; he also hears their cry and saves them'.

Mothers therefore need to continually teach children and those looking up to God to constantly remain in the place of prayer as God will surely hear and answer.

The Lord has promised us in Psalm 23:4 (KJV):

'4Yea, though I walk through the valley of the shadow of death, I will fear no evil: for thou art with me; thy rod and thy staff they comfort me.'

Meaning it doesn't matter what may befall a person, God will continually watch over everyone and every mother will need to have this faith to walk through any situation and carry with them the people looking up to them. Some situations that a mother faces may be very complex to sort out, but God has assured us in His word that He will see His children through. The mother ought to enlighten the people looking up to them with this fact, that He will always be with them.

In conclusion, mothers need to fear God as this is what God's expectation is for every mother. The love of God, reflected through Jesus Christ has the power to cast out any fear of man in its many shapes and forms such as fear of guiding people in loving one another, fear of being a peace advocate and many more, but rather ensures the mother is free to do God's will and purposes. The ultimate in a mother's love is the fear of God because it shows us His perfect love that casts out all fear of our situations. He really does have what's best for us. Mothers need to remain advocates for God's reverence in all their support and guidance to people looking up to them. When the fear of God is instilled so much in children and people looking up to mothers, there is a unique love of God and love for the people, that makes any wrong they may have said or done completely insignificant. Everyone who loves has been born of God and knows God.

To know God in the fear of Him as a wonder working God, full of awe, reverence, respect for Him our Holy Creator who died and paid the price.

This truth rests on the fact that God is the Almighty God and every man or woman is God's Child. Hence, it's important to identify and relate appropriately the coexisting truths that we have to have a true fear of God and realise His amazing love for us.

The Bible says in Psalm 118:4:' Let those who fear the LORD say: "His love endures forever" we will hold Him in reverential fear and see and experience His love'. Psalm 147:11: 'The LORD delights in those who fear him, who put their hope in his unfailing love'. Reverence for God is our highest priority in our adoration of who He is. It's based on the parent-child relationship, where we trust that our parent knows what is best for us.

'29O that there were such an heart in them, that they would fear me, and keep all my commandments always, that it might be well with them, and with their children for ever!' *(Deuteronomy 5:29 KJV).*

CHAPTER 10

HOW TO REMAIN A MOTHER OF INFLUENCE - KEEPING YOUR INTEGRITY

Integrity is so critical in a mother's life, more so a great attribute for a Christ centred life. Integrity according to the *Collins English Dictionary* says, 'If you have integrity, you are honest and firm in your moral principles'. It is also important to point out that the word Integrity comes from a Latin adjective INTEGER, meaning wholeness or complete. A person who is being made whole portrays a single focus on God. This essentially comes with qualities such as honesty with God and consistency of one's character. Therefore, we need to have a good understanding of integrity to ensure our words and our actions depict our goals.

Mothers, again I say, stand in the privileged position where they are actually sought after for advice and counsel constantly. It is important that mothers are true to themselves and are not a different person in many different circumstances. The Bible confirms to me in Proverbs 10:9 (ESV): 'Whoever walks in integrity walks securely, but he who makes his ways crooked will be found out'.

Integrity is a much spoken about concept and even claimed by many mothers but is worth exploring as an individual to ascertain how we can have integrity in all areas of our lives. I have chosen to explore this concept because God has entrusted us with such a privilege to lead as mothers so we need to take it seriously. We can do this by holding ourselves accountable to both God and people. A person of integrity is, therefore, the same both in private and in public and will stand by their views whatever the cost. They are single-minded in their pursuit of God and give Him their whole life, including the struggles.

Our true colours often come out when the pressure is on. Normally, during this time, how a mother responds will be based on the state of the heart. For instance, a mother's tone of voice and response should not be based on where they are but should reflect who they are at all times. To an authentic mother, they are not so much taken by fame or popularity. They do, however, believe in credibility. God has placed mothers in such an incredible position and he wants to use every mother, but they need to be credible, whose words and actions align and come across as consistency and not confusion. I believe integrity of character always supports success but where integrity of character is compromised, it is a matter of time before the success comes tumbling down. Proverbs 11:3 (ESV) confirms this by saying: 'The integrity of the upright guides them, but the crookedness of the treacherous destroys them.' God is not mocked, whatsoever a man sows, he shall reap. Hence, it is paramount for a mother to be sincere in her actions. It is very important to be faithful as a mother at all times, especially in private because this is what proves our integrity of character. To have a character of integrity is to remain loyal to the right principles at all times. This is basically adhering to Gods will at all times. A mother has a responsibility to keep connected with God in order to be a woman of integrity. There are a number of ways we can do this: keeping in step with the Holy Spirit as much as we can; being attentive to Him throughout the day, including Him in everything we do and being honest with Him about how we are feeling helps us to stay authentically in His will.

Another mark of integrity is being able to pick ourselves up when we fall down. Knowing that we will make mistakes and being able to bring them to God unashamedly helps us to live an honest life. Seeking the best way to move forward, God will honour our integrity and direct our steps.

A good test for a mother is doing a self-check perhaps on whether the decisions that are made in private will be the same decisions made when there is an audience. We are told by 2 Corinthians 8:21 (ESV): 'For we aim at what is honourable not only in the Lord's sight but also in the sight of man'.

Will a mother give sound, unbiased advice for instance about a relationship without taking sides or gossiping both when there is an audience and on a one to one? The people God has entrusted in a mother's care are God's special children and God is watching from heaven every mother's single action. Mothers, God cannot be mocked. The consequences of every action will always come to light and the only way to remain a mother of influence is to keep your integrity. For a mother to be respected and entrusted by many, she has to earn their trust. A mother who keeps her integrity will always be referred to as authentic. What an honourable virtue to be desired. The more you are a person of integrity, the greater your voice as a mother and the more people will gravitate towards you. As a mother, it is virtuous to be above reproach as we all know there are so many people looking to a mother's conduct and Hebrews 12:1 (ESV) puts it this way: 'Therefore, since we are surrounded by so great a cloud of witnesses, let us also lay aside every weight, and sin which clings so closely, and let us run with endurance the race that is set before us'. My prayer is that we will keep our focus and not be distracted easily.

Having people and children looking up to us creates an opportunity to show either integrity or lack of integrity, based on where we are at with God. Character is therefore really important in the life of a mother. The character of a mother is not about what she says she is, but who she really is. We need integrity of character to boldly advise based on God's guidance. The Bible puts it this way in Romans 12:2 (KJV): 'And be not conformed to this world: but be ye transformed by the renewing of your mind, that ye may prove what is that good, and acceptable, and perfect, will of God'.

When a mother stands on Christ the solid rock, and follows through to advice based on the perfect will of God, it is clear that sound guidance and instruction will be given and those in receipt of this support will actually be well protected with great foundations.

I implore mothers by the mercy of God not to conform to their environment if it does not depict who God is. I understand that this can sometimes be a lonely decision but it's actually better to make a God decision than what may seem a "good decision". For instance, it might seem a normal thing to participate in negative derogatory talk because one is looking for a sense of belonging and doesn't want to be the odd one out, but I say it is rather more important to get into offering Godly counsel about the matter, if the person desires it – if not, just be there to listen.

It looks like a hard thing to do, but it actually will bring joy and fulfilment to both the mother and the person being advised. It shouldn't matter the consequences. The Bible says in Romans 5:3-5 (ESV): 'More than that, we rejoice in our sufferings, knowing that suffering produces endurance, and endurance produces character, and character produces hope, and hope does not put us to shame, because God's love has been poured into our hearts through the Holy Spirit who has been given to us'.

If a mother can stand for what is right and not conform to the negative environment it actually reflects a true picture of maturity of character. I pray that all of us will not be scared to stand for the truth and not conform to the affairs of this world. Mothers then soon realise the benefits of obedience and leading people in the right direction. The people looking up to the mother will be able to have more regard and respect for such a mother. A mother who respects godly values is a woman of substance and her integrity will be sure because her actions are a true representation of her words.

Being a mother of integrity is not the easiest to remain. But with purpose, intent and self-motivation, integrity will be established.

Hebrews 12:2 (ESV) reminds us that: 'Looking to Jesus, the founder and perfecter of our faith, who for the joy that was set before him endured the cross, despising the shame, and is seated at the right hand of the throne of God'.

There is so much joy set before us when living a life of integrity. Jesus endured the pain and the suffering knowing the joy that was set before Him. I believe this helps in the process of building a strong character of integrity, if we don't give up.

The psalmist says in Psalm 25:21 (ESV): 'May integrity and uprightness preserve me, for I wait for you.' Beloved mothers, let's wait on the Lord. A good character is a great tool of integrity and will make you achieve your dreams, goals and aspirations in life.

A good strong character will give a mother a high level of integrity with which she advises her children and the people looking up to her. Mothers can be faced with difficult challenges that they need to make decisions over, but with integrity of heart, wise counsel will be given. Mothers ought to believe that, God who has called you, has also given you the courage to do according to Philippians 4:13 (ESV): 'I can do all things through him who strengthens me'.

Allowing God to work on our character is therefore essential for integrity and it will take endurance for it to be established. Integrity will sustain your character and keep your achievements and success at the top. Many people will aspire to be like you. Character cannot be claimed it has to be lived.

A mother needs be trustworthy. Mothers to me, seem to influence how people looking up to them make their decisions and I would like to believe that all of these are born from trust-worthy mothers. To me, a mother should be dependable, ethical and upright. As I have mentioned above, they stand by principles and are not seen as wavering. They are ready to make a decision based on their principles. We need to have values by which our lives are governed. We need to be mindful of the queue behind us that can be affected by the advice that comes out of our mouths. It is obvious that these decisions carry with them a ripple effect on many people and consequently, affecting families.

Proverbs 20:7 (ESV): 'The righteous who walks in his integrity— blessed are his children after him!'

Hence, depending on whether the advice is good or bad will determine the effect of the outcome.

Honesty is a value that we need to behold as mothers. There is an expectation from Gods word that mothers will be honest. Proverbs 6:16-20 (ESV) says: 'There are six things that the Lord hates, seven that are an abomination to him: haughty eyes, a lying tongue, and hands that shed innocent blood, a heart that devises wicked plans, feet that make haste to run to evil, a false witness who breathes out lies, and one who sows discord among brothers. My son, keep your father's commandment, and forsake not your mother's teaching'.

Mothers, let's teach right. Being honest and telling the truth is paramount so that we train those entrusted to us in the right manner. I don't believe in white lies and black lies as some people would put it, lying is lying full stop! A mother cannot be dishonest just a little bit and stand at 100% in the place of integrity. 'Do not lie to one another, seeing that you have put off the old self with its practices' *(Colossians 3:9 ESV)* whilst the book of Ephesians says it this way'

'Speaking the truth in love, we will grow to become in every respect the mature body of him who is the head, that is, *Christ*' *(Ephesians 4:15 ESV).*

One of the main ways we continue to speak the truth is to study God's word daily and apply it. The Bible confirms this in (Psalm 119:11 ESV): 'I have stored up your word in my heart, that I might not sin against you'.

Speaking the truth in love makes us trustworthy as mothers. Such a mother will remain a mother of influence due to her testimony of integrity.

A mother's integrity is a true testimony to some people of how genuine God is. Let our lives be a living testimony to everyone around. Mothers need to always remember that this is God's assignment for them and to always completely depend and rely on God for direction. I also encourage mothers to remember that whatever you do for those looking up to you, do not look to them for a reward. Do everything as unto God and not unto man. 'Whatever you do, work heartily, as for the Lord and not for men' *(Colossians 3:23 ESV).*

My prayer is that, as a mother, you will always be a woman of great character and will delight in speaking the truth, hence upholding your integrity. Don't be shaken or surprised when negative things are spoken about you, instead, pray and the Lord will vindicate you and honour you.

'Having a good conscience, so that, when you are slandered, those who revile your good behaviour in Christ may be put to shame' *(1 Peter 3:16 ESV).*

God is always looking for a mother of character and integrity, that He may entrust more lives in your care. When you are faithful in little, He will make you faithful in much *(Luke 16:10 ESV).*

'One who is faithful in a very little is also faithful in much, and one who is dishonest in a very little is also dishonest in much.'

When mothers have integrity, people looking up to them feel safe. They can trust you and so will God entrust more of His children in your care.

'Let not steadfast love and faithfulness forsake you; bind them around your neck; write them on the tablet of your heart' *(Proverbs 3:3 ESV)*.

Mothers, let's remember that everything that we are able to do is because of the grace of God over our lives.

Philippians 2:13 (ESV) says: 'For it is God who works in you, both to will and to work for his good pleasure'.

When we help people, let's remember, all the glory, honour and gratitude belongs to God.

REFERENCES

CPSIA information can be obtained
at www.ICGtesting.com
Printed in the USA
BVHW030435020419
544227BV00033B/139/P

9 781786 234964